The Early Family Home

Bobbie Kalman

The Early Settler Life Series

Crabtree Publishing Company
Toronto
New York

To my Father, who gave me my ambition.

A very special thanks to:

My excellent editorial, research, and layout staff: Lise Gunby, Nancy Cook, Rosemary McLernon and Nora Peat.

The expert photographers who are responsible for the faithful reproductions of old historical materials: Sarah Peters and Stephen Mangione.

The librarians and historians who were so cooperative in providing me with historical materials and photographic opportunities: William Loos, Margaret Crawford Maloney, Dana Tenny, Jill Shefrin, Christine Castle, Margaret Perkins, Nan Wronski, Gabriella Karadi, Tom Nagy and Bill Logan.

My talented, beautiful and very patient models: Samantha and Andrea Crabtree.

Copyright © 1982, 1990, 1992 Crabtree Publishing Company

Cataloging in Publication Data

Kalman, Bobbie, 1947 –
   The early family home

(Early settler life series)
Includes index.
ISBN 0-86505-017-1 hardcover
ISBN 0-86505-016-3 softcover

1. Home economics – History. 2. Frontier and pioneer life. I. Title. II. Series.

TX19.K34   *640'.9'03*   LC 93-30699

350 Fifth Ave, Suite 3308
New York, NY 10118

R.R. #4
360 York Road
Niagara-on-the-Lake, ON
Canada L0S 1J0

73 Lime Walk
Headington, Oxford 0X3 7AD
United Kingdom

Contents

In the first years of a settler's new life the shanty and log cabin are built. Behind the cabin there is a small field of crops ready to be harvested. The settler's second field, in front, is now being cleared of logs.

Chopping their way to civilization

The earliest settlers actually had to carve their new lives out of the forest. Trees covered most of the land. The only way to make a home was to chop down the trees and clear an area. The next task was to erect a shanty, lean-to, or tent. Once the temporary shelter was up, more ground would be cleared for the log cabin. After it was built, the settler had to plant crops right away so that the family would have food to eat when the supplies they had brought with them ran out. Clearing the land for fields took a long time. But slowly the trees came down and the crops went in. Fences were built and roads were made. By the time the children of the settlers were grown up, they would no longer be living in a log cabin. They would enjoy a comfortable life in a large two-story home made of planks, bricks, or stones.

Fifteen years later fences separate the fields. The stumps are gone. The settlers live in a two-story house made of squared logs. There is a barn for the animals and a corduroy bridge made of logs over the stream.

Thirty-five years later the settlers are living in a large plank house. The new bridge is also made of planks. There are several barns. The settler is now also the sawmill owner.

Marcus brings more firewood to Mother, who is busy cooking our first supper in the bush.

Samantha Stell shares her settler story

The Stell family came to their new home in the forest in the summer of 1817. Charles Stell's brother, Peter, also emigrated with the family. Charles and Caroline Stell had five children: Samantha, Marcus, John, Edith, and Amy. Samantha was the oldest child. She was 14. This story has been written as it would have been told by Samantha. The characters are not real. However, the information and poems are. They have been taken from letters and diaries written by real settlers.

Rest for weary travelers

It was almost nightfall when we arrived at a place where we could spend the night. We came upon a small clearing in the forest which Father found suitable for making our beds. We had traveled all day over bumpy dirt roads in a wagon pulled by a team of oxen. We were all tired and a little discouraged. The two small children were beyond caring. They were fast asleep hours ago. It was up to Marcus and me to find firewood quickly, while Father, John, and Uncle Peter tried to make our sleeping place as comfortable as possible. They chopped some hemlock boughs. They placed the larger evergreen branches in a circle to keep out the wind, and made our beds of the smaller boughs. Mother cooked us a small supper of potatoes on the fire Marcus and I had made, after which we were all thankful to get some rest.

Right down to work

After one more day of travel we finally reached our land. The place where our house and fields would be was a dense forest beside a lake. Fortunately, we were able to find shelter at the home of a Mr. Adams, who, it seems, was to be our nearest neighbor. We slept comfortably in beds that night, the first time in more than three weeks.

When we woke the next morning, we had to begin building our shanty right away. Mr. Adams and a few more of our new neighbors came along to lend us a hand. Everyone, including my small sisters, helped by chopping trees, gathering branches, and cutting bark off the logs. Before nightfall the next day, the men had finished building a shanty. The walls were made of logs, and the roof of bark. Beside the shanty they erected a shed for cooking. Marcus and I quickly made a fire-pit. We cooked our very first meal that night. We constructed a frame of green wood which held our pots and kettles over the fire.

Marcus looks ready to enjoy his sleep in the first comfortable bed he has had in three weeks. Neighbors offered us a place to stay.

Our log cabin was finished in no time with the help of our kind neighbors. Uncle Peter and John take a break from cutting the logs that will soon become Mother's new cupboard.

Busy builders

Our neighbors dropped in to help us in any way they could. They chopped down trees to clear land for our first crops. Mother and Mrs. Adams planted seeds for corn, squash, carrots, pumpkins, and peas. Amy, Edith, and John helped to put the seeds into the earth. They were very excited to be at their new home. They played hide-and-seek among the many trees and leap-frogged over the tree stumps. They discovered a brook nearby in which Edith happily cooled her toes. Nothing seemed to bother their playful little world.

Marcus and I were busy collecting branches, chopping underbrush, and swatting flies and mosquitoes. It seemed that every inch of my body was covered in itchy red welts. But the little ones did not complain of the heat or the bugs. Oh, how I envied their sense of carefree adventure!

Impressions in poetry

Marcus, the poet of our family, wrote down his first thoughts on our new home. He showed his poem to us after supper that evening.

Cutting the first tree

We cut the trees that were so handy,
We soon put up our little shanty,
On a point round which the lake
Wound like an enormous snake,
As if it would bind it fast,
Then it stretched away at last.
We were awkward at the ax,
And the trees were stubborn facts,
I mind a sturdy elm well,
'Twas the first we tried to fell,
I could point you out, I know,
The very spot where it did grow.

I liked Marcus' poem. However, not to be outdone by my younger brother, I also wrote down my first impressions of our days in the backwoods.

Work!

Work! for the night is coming;
Work! through the morning hours;
Work! while the dew is sparkling;
Work! 'mid the springing flowers;
Work! while the day grows brighter,
Under the flowing sun;
Work! for the night is coming,
Night – when our work is done.
Work! for the night is coming;
Work! through the sunny noon,
Fill the bright hours with labor;
Rest cometh sure and soon.
Give to each flying minute
Something to keep in store;
Work! for the night is coming;
Night – when we work no more.

My poem caused a lot of laughter. My Mother said that I always managed to see the practical side of everything. As we curled up on the floor of our shanty that night, we all felt a sense of closeness that we had never known before as a family. Yes, we were working hard, but our work was filled with hope, togetherness, and a lot of love. We were creating a new life for ourselves. Our feelings for our new home grew with every passing hour.

Edith cools her toes in the brook while John and Amy examine an interesting rock.

Mother tells John and Amy a bedtime story by the fire. Father enjoys a puff on his pipe. The rest of us were sitting outside gazing at the beautiful stars.

Neighbors lend a hand

Once the work on the shanty was completed it was time to begin building our log house. Neighbors from all directions arrived at our shanty that day. Every hand was occupied in helping to raise our new home. Logs were felled and cut to the same length. Notches were made at both ends and the logs were laid in position, ready to be made into walls. The fireplace was started. The foundation was carefully built up of stones and the chimney was erected above it. The hearth was made.

Our cabin takes shape

The walls of the log cabin quickly went up. The notched end of one log fit nicely into the notched end of the next log, which was laid on top at right angles. The roof of our cabin was made of smaller logs and pieces of bark. After the roof had been completed, all that was left to do was to stuff moss, leaves, and mud into the spaces between the logs so that the wind and rain could not get through the cracks. We had no glass, so we pasted paper over our windows. The paper had been oiled so that light could pass through it. We hung a blanket over the doorway. We did not have the tools needed to make a door or hinges.

A new cupboard for Mother

We also had no furniture, but Uncle Peter was clever with his hands, and before too long, he had built bunk beds right into the walls of the cabin. He made tables out of wooden crates and chairs out of barrels. With his help, we all built our own stools. We made the seats by cutting thick slabs from the tops of tree trunks. Uncle Peter also built a cupboard for Mother. We had a hard time hiding it from her until it was finished. When she saw it, she cried with joy. Once again

While I was washing the dishes one night Marcus thought of another poem. He started to write it down, but would not tell me what it was about.

she could display her beautiful dishes
that she had brought with her from home.

Home at last

The Sunday after our cabin was finished
we read the Bible together. We thanked
the Lord for giving us the strength,
courage, and determination we needed to
build our home in the wilderness. We
thanked Him for the help and support our
kind new neighbors had given us in our
hard labors. But most of all, we thanked
Him for allowing us to be together. For
we had discovered that the love we felt for
each other could overcome any hardship.

After we had finished our prayers, Marcus
announced that he had a surprise for us.
He had written another poem. Uncle Peter
helped him to mount and frame it. We
hung it on the wall as our official housewarming symbol. As soon as the poem was
up, we knew we were truly "home" at last.

Our log cabin

*Our little log cabin is far in the woods,
The foot of the traveler seldom comes here;
Around it are stretching the great solitudes,
Where the deer love to roam, and the wolf
makes his lair,
And the dead tree falls with a heavy crash,
And the jagged hemlock and the pine are
there,
And the dismal swamp and the dreary ash,
And the eagle sits watching the moment to
dash.*

*The little log cabin is all alone,
Its windows are rude, and its walls are bare,
And the wind without has a weary moan;
Yet peace, like an angel is nestling there,
And hope with her rapt uplifted air,
Beholds in the distance the sweetbriar rose,
And the corn with its silver tassel where
The hemlock is anchored beside the tall pine,
And the creeping weed hangs with its long
fringing vine.*

Family members spend most of their time gathered around the fire where they enjoy warmth and companionship. Grandma has the warmest spot in the fireplace seat. In the winter the fireplace was the only source of heat in the settler home.

The fireplace

The settlers soon discovered that much of their time was spent in front of their fireplace. The fireplace provided light, warmth, and heat for cooking. Some of the earliest fireplaces were so large that the settlers built seats inside them. Most of the heat from the fire went up the chimney. The pioneers had to sit very close to the fireplace, or even inside it, in order to keep warm in the winter.

Borrowed fire

A huge log of wood was kept burning night and day. This glowing log was buried deep in ashes each night. In the morning, one simply had to blow on it with the bellows to start it flaming again. Settlers were careful not to allow the fire to go out completely. If the fire went out, no cooking could be done until it was started again - and their were no

Maggie set up her spinning wheel next to the fireplace so that she can stay warm as she works. She can cook her dinner and card wool at the same time. She is cooking savory stew flavored with some of the herbs that dry above the fireplace.

matches! Without matches it was very difficult to start another fire. It was easier to "borrow" fire from a nearby neighbor. Children were sent to get a burning coal and had to bring it back before it went out. This coal was carried in a pot or held between pieces of wood. One settler woman sent her daughter, Louise, to a neighbor's house when she found that her fire had gone out overnight.

Burnt shingles, burnt fingers

"Taking two dry wooden shingles, Louise set out for the nearest neighbor's house and there obtained a lump of glowing charcoal out of their buried log. This she held between her shingles very firmly and started home full speed, holding her shingles out at arm's length in front of her. Of course the faster she ran, the greater the draft of air on the charcoal, which immediately burned up and then set the shingles alight."

Louise had to be careful how quickly she walked with the burning coal. If the wind was blowing too hard, she might not have been able to get home before the coal burned the shingles and her hands!

The hired hand ordered our servant, Thomas, to set fires in a number of spots in the field. Little did we know how little Thomas knew!

Clearing the land

In order to clear the land around a home, the settler had to chop the trees, pull the stumps, and burn the bushes. When burning off a field, one had to be very careful how the fires were set. If the wind was blowing in the wrong direction, the whole forest could go up in flames.

Suzanna Moodie, an early settler, hired a man to help clear the land around her home. The man had never fired a field before, as she later found out the hard way! Suzanna Moodie's exciting story has been adapted slightly for your enjoyment.

Fire in the fallow

"I had never seen a fallow burnt, but I had heard about it so many times that I never realized it could be dangerous. Imagine my surprise and horror when on going to the back door, I saw that the fellow, to make sure of his work, had set the field alight in fifty places. Behind, before, on every side, we were surrounded by a wall of fire, burning furiously within a hundred meters of us, and cutting off all possibility of escape ...

"I closed the door, and went back to the kitchen. Fear was knocking loudly at my heart. Our utter helplessness took away all hope of making an escape - I was in shock!

"I grew strangely calm after my initial fear. Tears were useless; we were facing a horrible death; and yet I could not believe we were going to die. I sat down on the doorstep, and watched the awful scene in silence. The fire was raging in the cedar swamp immediately below the ridge on which the house stood ...

No escape

"There was thick smoke all around. The air was filled with fiery sparks which floated down right to the doorstep. The crackling and roaring of the flames must have been heard at a great distance ...

"The fierce wind drove the flames at the sides and back of the house up the clearing, and our passage to the road was completely cut off by a sea of flames. The only safe place was the house, so long as it remained untouched by the fire. I turned to young Tom and asked him how long he thought it would be before the flames reached the house.

"'When the fire clears this little ridge in front, ma'am. The Lord have mercy upon us, for then we must all go!'

We needed a miracle

"The heat soon became suffocating. We were parched with thirst. There was not a drop of water in the house, and none could be brought from the lake. I turned once more to the door, hoping to see a way out. I saw nothing but a dense cloud of fire and smoke. I could hear nothing but crackling and roaring. The flames were gaining so fast upon us that I felt their scorching breath in my face ...

"The wind rose to a hurricane, scattering the flames on all sides. The willows swayed in fiery agony. I buried my head in my apron, for I thought that all was lost. A most terrific crash of thunder burst over our heads. Down came the rushing torrent of rain which had been pent up for many weeks. In a few minutes the chip-yard was all afloat, and the fire was nothing more than a hiss of steam."

Prairie fires

Fires were not just a threat to those who lived in the forest. The prairie settlers also faced the danger of losing their homes and lives in a prairie fire. Prairie fires came regularly every autumn as soon as the grass turned brown and dry. A prairie fire often started because of a careless settler. It spread very quickly, destroying the crops and homes in its path.

Elizabeth tried desperately to keep the creature out. Fortunately for her, the bear did not attempt coming into our house. A door would have been no barrier against a big bear.

The bear break-in

The settlers who lived in the woods had both friendly and unfriendly visitors. Below is a true story of a middle-of-the-night visit from an uninvited guest. The story is told in the settler's own words.

"In the middle of the night my wife and her sister were awakened and very frightened by a terrible noise in the kitchen, accompanied by the sharp barking of the little dog. They were quite sure by the low growls and the fury of Suffolk the dog, that it was some wild animal, but whether it was a bear or a wolf they could not tell. Towards morning, this unwelcome visitor took himself off, to their infinite joy. When I came home, they told me the story. I laughed very heartily, for I thought their fears had magnified the visit of some neighbor's dog into a bear or some other wild beast. Both were convinced they were right.

We barely escaped

"Before going to bed, I loaded my gun and tied Suffolk up near the pork barrel. At midnight we were suddenly awakened by the pitiful howling of the poor dog. There was a loud noise that sounded as if everything in the room had been violently thrown down. I jumped out of bed instantly, and seizing my gun, crept carefully along the passage, till I came to the kitchen door, which I threw open. Some large, dark-looking object made a rush for the unfinished part of the floor. I immediately fired, but it was so dark and the beast so quick, that I had little chance of hitting him ...

"As soon as the beast had made his exit, we lighted a candle and examined the room, which we found in confusion and disorder ... From what I can make out of the footprints outside I am inclined to think my unwelcome visitor was a bear."

The bear was so quick that I had no chance of hitting him. Suffolk growled in his most vicious tone after he was sure the animal had left.

The bear returned a few weeks later. He met his end on the night that he tried to rip the door off our storage shed.

Ben helps his father to build a rail fence. Fences were important because they kept the animals of the settlers on their own properties.

18

Friendly settlers built stiles into their fences so that their neighbors could easily cross their property. These girls know their neighbors are friendly. However, they are not certain that their horses are!

Friendship fences

As soon as the settlers began raising their own animals, fences were a must. They had to keep their animals in and other animals out. It was believed that a friendship with a neighbor was only as strong as the fences separating the two properties. Rail fences were the most popular farm fences. However, settlers made fences out of whatever wood was around. Some settlers made their fences out of tree stumps that were pulled out of their fields.

Settlers often walked across each other's property because it was the shortest route to the village or mill. Good neighbors built stiles into their fences so that people could easily get over them. Animals, however, could not get through the stiles. Neighbors sometimes met at the stiles for a friendly chat.

These young neighbors find the stile a perfect place to meet. Each of them would still be considered "at home", so there would be no need for a chaperone.

19

These western settlers chose to make their home on the bank of a river. They could easily row their boat to the general store or catch a steamboat to the nearby city.

Rivers, lakes, and springs

There were few roads in the early days. To go to the nearest town or gristmill often meant walking for many days. However, if a settler lived near a river or a lake, a trip to church or to market could be made much faster by boat. Living near water also assured the settler of plenty of water for drinking, bathing and laundry. One settler explained why her family chose to live near a spring.

"Where water is, there a habitation will be; where a river is, there a town will appear. Our spring was under a little ledge of rock, rather narrow and not very deep. It rose up from underneath and was nearly always full. A small streamlet trickled away from it down to the creek some distance away. Now as long as the streamlet trickled, all was well with us. We could dip our pails and come again, certain of finding the spring filled up, clean, clear and cool."

The water at our little spring was always clear, clean, and cool.

The pioneers, above, settled on the shores of a lake. They also dug a well in front of their home. Carrying water was a tiring chore which often caused back injuries.

Wells

Some settlers could get their water from a nearby spring. However, carrying water was a backbreaking job. Most of the settlers would dig a well near the house as soon as they could. Settlers had many ideas about where water was located on their property. One of the favorite ways to look for water was to carry a willow switch around the property. When the end of it pulled down towards the ground, it was believed there would be water there. Some people made money from locating water for others. They traveled from farm to farm with their *divining rods* offering their services.

Once a likely spot was found, the settlers dug until they reached water. They lined the inside of the well with stones. Sometimes the hole in the ground was covered up with a board. More often, however, stones were built up in a circle around the well so that no one would fall into it.

Lisa and Debbie stop for a chat at the well. This type of well was called a sweep well. The bucket was lowered into the well by means of the pole. When the handle was raised, the bucket at the other end reached down into the water. The handle was then lowered to the ground again to bring up the full bucket.

21

Samantha remembers her first months in the small log cabin. She is living in a large plank house now. The family has added on to the home since she married. There is enough room for everyone, including the children Samantha plans to have.

Plank houses for more comfort

Once the log cabin was built, the barn and fences were put up, and the land around the house was cleared of logs, the settlers started to think about building a better home. This home was not made of logs. It was a plank house. Planks could be cut by hand from squared logs, but it was a lengthy job. It was easier to buy planks from a nearby sawmill. The later settlers who set up homes near towns or cities built plank houses right away.

Plank houses were usually two stories high. The downstairs contained the kitchen, the dining room, and the parlor. In some houses there was an extra room near the kitchen called the "borning room". It was called that because the children of the house were born there. The borning room was usually the parents' bedroom. The smaller children of the family often slept there with the parents. Because it was next to the kitchen, it was the second warmest room in the house.

Upstairs in the plank house would be three or four bedrooms. The bedrooms were heated by the pipes which carried the smoke from the kitchen and living room stoves up to the chimney. There were usually two chimneys in the roof. The roof of the plank house was made of shingles instead of logs. Shingles were made at the sawmill.

The kitchen of the plank house often contained a stove instead of a fireplace. Stoves were more useful than fireplaces. They did not let all the heat escape up the chimney. The heat stayed in the room. Stoves were also easier to cook on than fireplaces. Lighter pots and pans could be used instead of the heavy kettles and big iron pots.

Getting the planks for their houses from the sawmill saved the settlers a lot of hard work and time. The sawmill also served another important function. Usually there was a finishing mill next to the sawmill, where rough boards were made smooth. A cabinetmaker could use this smooth wood for making good furniture. The cabinetmaker could then sell this furniture to the settlers for their new plank houses.

Andrea finds her candle-making chore much easier to accomplish on a stove.

The interior walls of the plank house were often decorated with bright wallpaper. The floors were made of smooth, painted boards.

The picture above shows four kinds of beds: a cradle, a turn-up bed, a trundle bed, and a canopy bed. Read the information on beds. Can you identify each one? Which bed is supported by rope?

The first beds were built right into the walls of the log cabins. A platform of wood and a scattering of straw made up the mattress.

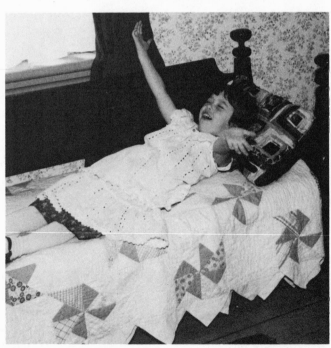

Katie enjoys her rest on an old-fashioned couch bed. Notice the pretty handmade quilt.

Beds, beds, beds

The early settlers made their beds of wood and rope. The frame and the legs of the bed were carved out of the wood. Holes were bored through the four sides of the frame. Rope was pulled through the holes, forming a strong net. A mattress of straw was placed on top of this rope network. After a person had slept on the bed for a few weeks, the rope would begin to sag in the middle. A small child was then asked to walk around the outer part of the frame to pull the network tight again. In later days a special tool was used to tighten the rope.

Trundle beds were found in many homes. These were low beds on wheels. Trundle beds could be pushed under a higher bed during the day and pulled out at night. These beds allowed the settlers to have more space during the day. In order to save space, settlers also changed benches and drawers into children's beds at night. One of the best space-saving beds was the *turn-up* bed. It was built into the wall at one end. The far end could be turned up and attached to the same wall. It saved a lot of room during the day. The room could be used as a workroom or sewing-room by day and as a bedroom by night. As the settlers built bigger and better houses, the beds also became fancier and more comfortable. *Canopy* beds with fringes, valances and curtains hanging around them were popular with the richer settlers.

Mattresses were made from corn husks, boughs, straw, hay, and goose feathers. Most settlers kept geese. The geese were plucked while they were still alive. The feathers grew back. The feathers of the geese were put inside a large bag made of rough ticking fabric. Straw was placed on the other side of the feathers. This bag became the mattress. The straw side was up in summer and the feather side was up in winter. The feathers kept the settlers warm and the straw kept them cool. The early settlers covered themselves with buffalo hides and bear skins. Then quilts were used as covers. The later settlers bought or made sheets and pillow cases for a more comfortable sleep.

Sometimes the settlers' children had to sleep in drawers and benches if there were not enough beds to go around.

The later settlers enjoyed sleeping between sheets of linen and under warm comforters. However, the more comfortable the bed, the more difficult it was to make it.

25

Mother plays the piano for Katherine in the parlor. The family's most prized possessions were kept there.

The parlor

The parlor was the special room in the home. It was usually the room in which guests were entertained. In many houses the parlor was not used at other times. If the settlers owned a piano, it would be kept in the parlor. The best furniture in the house would be found in the parlor. Women also did their needlework there. On Sundays the family read the Bible in the parlor. Special guests were always shown to the parlor and were served tea there.

When a girl was old enough to date, the young man was invited to "court" her in the parlor. A date in those days usually meant playing the piano for the young man while the grandmother sat in a chair knitting. It was not considered proper for young people to be alone together without a *chaperone*. The chaperone made sure the young people acted properly on their date.

On Sunday the children read the Bible in the parlor.

Some ladies did their fine needlework, such as needlepoint, in the parlor. The best wallpaper and carpets graced that room. It was peaceful there.

The old etching, above, was entitled "Our parlor borders". The room called the parlor was where young people "courted" or met with their dates. The artist who drew these young people must have thought of the meadow as their outdoor parlor because the young men were courting the ladies there.

Bathrooms, indoors and out

Instead of indoor plumbing, the settlers used outdoor facilities. The outhouse, above, is a luxury model. It has a big window and two seats.

Chamber pots were used for nighttime emergencies.

The settlers washed their faces and hands in a basin each morning and night. The pitcher of water stood waiting to be used.

The messy wash-up

When Tom begins to wash himself,
 The mess he makes is frightful!
And yet the naughty boy declares
 That messing is delightful.

He'll fill that basin to the brim,
 Till water trickles under,
Or else the water-jug itself
 Is sure to break asunder.

These duckies were made of wood.

Old-fashioned fun!

The best way to learn about the early family home is to explore one yourself. Every city has at least one or two. Find the historic houses in your area and pay a visit soon. You'll find a new way to have fun in an old world.

What could be more fun than a bath by the fireplace in an old-fashioned tub?

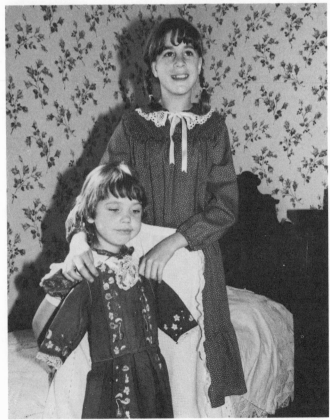

I don't think this dress suits me.

Is anybody in there?

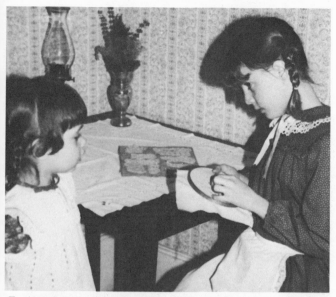

Embroidery anyone?

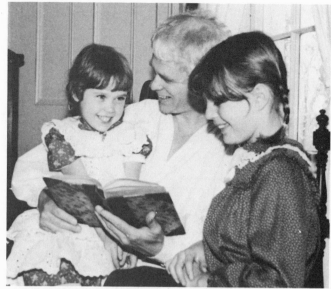

What a funny story!

Knead that bread!

What to take for an awful toothache?

Yummy peppermint sticks from the general store.

We've found old things that were once new; we've had lots of fun sharing them with you.

Tommy gets his daily dose of tonic. It tastes horrible! His mother believes that the more bitter the tonic tastes, the better it is for preventing illness.

Sharing their germs

The early settlers knew very little about medicine compared to what we know today. They knew nothing about germs or how disease was spread. Often many people drank from one cup and used the same plate and spoon. When a traveler stopped at an inn, for example, there was usually one towel, comb, and washbowl to be shared by all the guests. Often strangers slept together in one room and even had to share a bed with one or two others.

Things were not much better in the home. People did not bathe very often. They believed that bathing washed away important body oils that prevented illness. Clothes were seldom washed. When people washed either themselves or their clothes, the dirty water was often thrown right outside the door of the house. Sometimes the water seeped into the nearby well and made the well water dirty. The settlers then drank the water and became ill. They did not know why they were ill.

Doctors knew little

Some people believed that new areas were free of disease. They did not realize that it was people, not land, that carried the diseases. Doctors were not much wiser about disease. Patients were made to bleed when the doctor scratched their skin with an instrument called a *fleam*. Bleeding was a popular treatment although it often made people weak and sometimes killed them. *Poultices* or pastes made of various herbs were often applied to areas of the body where people felt pain. Tonics of all kinds were made in the home and sold at the general store. It was believed that the more bitter the tonic, the better the cure.

Herbal remedies

There were not many doctors in the backwoods settlements. Sometimes it took a doctor the better part of a day to reach a patient. For this reason, people tried to cure themselves at home. Many plants, roots, and flowers were used as medicines. These herbs were planted as soon as a settler reached the new homestead. There were two kinds of herbal remedies. *Simples* were used to cure illnesses. *Benefits* were like vitamins. They were taken to keep the settlers healthy.

Horehound was boiled and the liquid used to relieve sore throats. It was believed that celery seeds were good for curing rheumatism. The root of spignet was made into a cough syrup and hop tea was believed to relieve indigestion. Nerve-vine roots were chewed to soothe the nerves. Herbs were a part of every pioneer kitchen. They were usually hung to dry on the ceiling near the fireplace or stove.

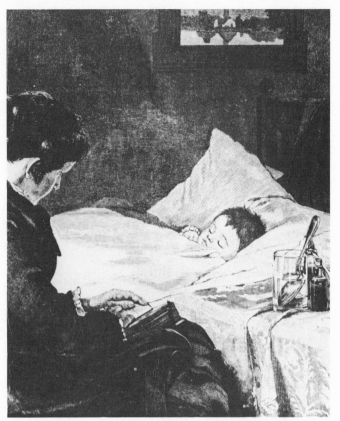

The mother in the picture, above, sits up all night with her sick child. She prays his fever will break by morning. Children were often sick in the old days.

The settlers grew herbs as soon as they arrived. These herbs have been hung to dry in the pantry. Some will be used in cooking, and others made into medicine.

33

Settlers lived with their extended families. An extended family included not only a mother, a father, and children, but also included grandparents, aunts, and uncles. Sometimes as many as four generations of people lived in one home.

Settlers had large families

The children of the settlers often followed in their parents' footsteps. The father in the picture above is teaching his son how to make a net. The son will learn to be a fisherman, just as his dad is.

Grandfathers were fun to live with. The one in the picture, above, is telling his grandson of his experiences in battle. The old days come to life again with the sound of a drum roll. The boy feels as if he were a real soldier!

Grandmother and Grandfather take a quiet moment to remember their first days in their log cabin. They have built a large plank house where they now live with their son and his family. The grandchildren are coming home from school soon and the house will once again be filled with shouts and laughter. Until the children come, only the grandparents' voices can be heard in the still farmhouse.

Grandfather has brought his favorite grandchild a doll from the city. Eve, however, is much more interested in her grandfather's pocket watch. He has promised her that it will someday belong to one of her children.

Most children were taught how to knit by the age of four. This little girl is being shown how by her mother. She will soon be able to make her own hats, scarves, and sweaters.

Picking berries was considered children's work. Children did not mind this job one bit. They could sing, talk, enjoy the sunshine, and eat all the berries they wanted. The signs of a successful day were pails full of berries and bright red or blue mouths and teeth!

Apples were one of the most important foods for the settler. Every hand was occupied in gathering, peeling, and coring the apples. The children especially loved to work outside.

Looking after the smaller animals was usually the job of one of the children. Little Nora protects her ducklings from an unfriendly chicken.

Everyone worked around the pioneer home. There was water to fetch, cows to milk, chickens to feed, and eggs to collect. Some jobs were harder than others, and some were more dangerous! One of the most dangerous was trying to get around the geese in the yard. Geese were menacing and vicious. But Suzie goes on with her morning chores armed with a big stick.

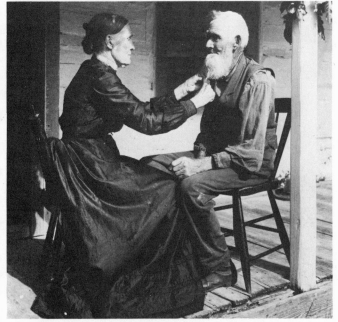

The settlers did not go to barbers or hairdressers. Grandmother or Grandfather usually had the job of giving haircuts and trimming beards.

In this family even the children had to wash their own clothes by hand. Their mother was still weak from a long illness. She sat near the children to make sure they did a good job.

The tallow from bayberries was made into a wonderfully fragrant candle.

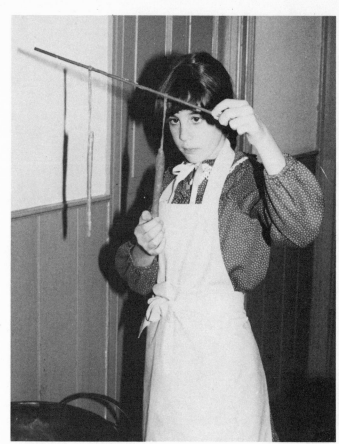

One way to make candles was to dip wicks again and again into melted tallow.

Ouch! I scratched my finger on the candle mold again.

Making candles is a hateful chore!

Making candles

Candle-making was a chore most children hated. It was messy and took a lot of patience. This is how candles were made. Pieces of loosely spun hemp were dipped into saltpeter and then twisted. The hemp was then doubled, leaving a loop at one end. These pieces of string served as wicks for the candles. (Ready-made wicks could later be bought from peddlers or at the general store.) The candle rod was slipped through the loops of ten or twenty wicks. Several rods full of hanging wicks were lowered into the hot wax rod by rod. Children usually had the job of dipping the wicks, taking them out to dry, dipping the next set of wicks, and so on. Many dippings were necessary to get candles thick enough to last at least one evening.

A greasy mess

The wax used by the settlers was made in the home. Every bit of animal and vegetable fat was saved for candle and soap-making. Bayberries and beeswax were also used in making candles. Even moose fat and bear oil were used. Candle wax was made by boiling the fat in water until the water boiled away and the dirt was skimmed off. This boiling fat into which the wicks were dipped was called *tallow*. When homemade candles burned, the smell was similar to frying grease.

A hateful chore

Another way settlers made candles was by pouring hot tallow into candle molds made of pewter or tin. These molds were set in a frame. Some of the frames held as many as 100 candle molds. A young pioneer girl shares her feelings about candle-making with us:

"One domestic job which went hard with me was candle-making. Why I should have so disliked it I cannot now very clearly understand; maybe it was because in my awkwardness I scalded my fingers in the boiling fat, or scratched them when putting the wicks into the molds. Anyhow I hated it, and let everyone know the fact."

It seems that only the mice looked forward to candle-making time. They found the tallow candles delicious for nighttime nibbling.

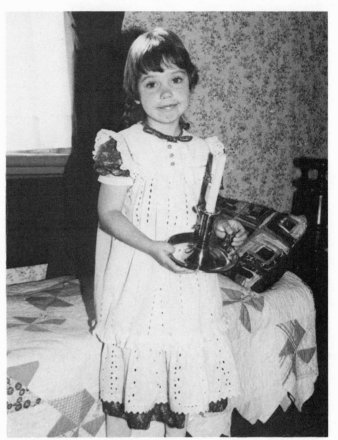

All that work and what do I get? A candle with which to go right to bed.

While the children sleep, the mice enjoy a nighttime nibble of homemade candle.

The first step in soap-making is melting scraps of fat into tallow.

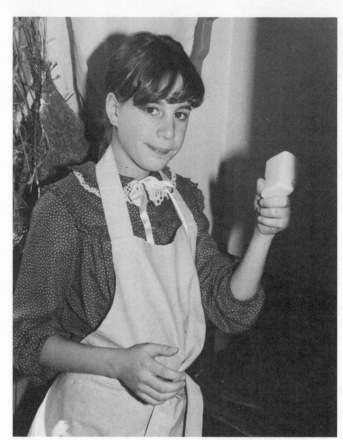

Homemade soap, ready for use.

Katie washes her hands with the soap Mother has just made. Andrea pours water into the basin for her.

Homemade soap was also used for shaving, washing hair, doing laundry, and bathing.

Making soap

Although soap could be bought at the general store, most settlers preferred to make their own. Basic soap was made from lye and grease. Other ingredients, such as borax, ammonia, resin, wild ginger leaves, and tallow of bayberry, were sometimes added.

Clean soap from dirty old ashes

Lye was made from ashes. Every pioneer had an abundance of ashes because of all the trees that were burned down around the homestead. The ashes were placed in a barrel, called a leach, which was put on top of a board. The board was raised at one end. The bottom of the barrel had a narrow slit which allowed water to seep through. A bucket was placed under the slit. As the water passed through the ashes, it trickled out as lye. Often it took a day for the first drops of lye to drip through the bottom of the barrel. Lye was very dangerous. It could burn the skin badly and burn the throat if the fumes were breathed. Children were not allowed to stay around when soap was being made.

Tallow tames lye

Animal fat and water were boiled in a large kettle. The lye was added to the melted fat. The melted fat was called *tallow*. The tallow took away the strength of the lye. Both the lye and the tallow were boiled together over a fire, usually outdoors. Bayberry tallow was added to the grease and lye for bath soap. Ammonia and borax were added for laundry soap. The liquid soap was poured into a pan or box and allowed to harden overnight. The next day it was cut into bars ready for use.

Potash

Many settlers made potash. Potash was in great demand by soap manufacturers in the cities of North America and Europe. Making potash was a good way for a settler to earn extra money. Potash was solid lye which had been boiled down in a huge iron pot and allowed to cool into a solid. It was sold in this solid form. The name "potash" comes from the joining of the two words, "pot" and "ash". Some of the settlers sold their ashes to the storekeeper. The storekeeper made the ashes into potash and exported the potash in large quantities.

Potash made by the settlers was exported to Europe. It was used by companies, such as Pears, to make brand name soaps.

The McKay sisters crowd the log cabin with the tools and machines used to make fabric from raw wool. Katy, on the left, pulls tangled bunches of wool between two carding boards which have wire teeth to comb the wool. Elaine, on the right, spins the wool into thread. Sheila sits at the loom weaving the threads into wool material.

Settlers made their own clothes

The early settlers had to make most of their own clothes. Some clothes were made from the skins of animals, such as deer, raccoon, squirrel, rabbit, bear, and buffalo. The hides of the animals became leather after they were *tanned*. The skins were stretched out to dry in the sun. They were soaked in a solution of hemlock and oak bark for a few weeks until the flesh and hair came off. The raw hide was then pounded with sticks and kneaded by hand for a softer texture.

Many of the backwoods settlers made their clothes of leather and fur. Breeches, buckskin coats, mittens, and raccoon hats kept the settlers warm. One little girl made a beautiful coat of rabbit, squirrel,

and raccoon pelts all sewn together. It was colorful and kept out the cold. The first settlers also made their own shoes of leather.

Wool from sheep

Most of the settlers' clothing, however, was made from wool, linen, or a combination of the two called *linsey-woolsey*. Wool came from sheep. In the spring the sheep were taken down to the nearby creek or river to be washed in water and a tobacco solution. The tobacco killed the bugs which lived in the wool. The sheep were washed so that their wool would be as clean as possible. Children loved to help wash the sheep because after the last animal was out of the water, they could swim, splash, and play in the creek for hours.

The next day every able hand was used to shear the wool off the sheep and to sort out the clean wool from the dirty wool. The wool was greased and rolled up. It was then *carded* or untangled. The settlers in the backwoods carded their own wool by pulling it between two carding boards. If the settlers lived near a town, the wool was taken to a carding mill where it was quickly and cheaply carded by machines. After the wool was carded it was spun into yarn on a large wheel sometimes called a *monster wheel*. The person who operated the wheel had to walk three steps forward to attach the wool to the spindle and then three steps back. Some pioneers walked as much as 30 km a day while spinning. The yarn was wound onto the reel into coils of wool called *skeins*. The skeins of wool were dyed in different colors. This was done by putting the skeins into hot dye.

Dying the wool

Dyes were made from barks, nuts, flowers, roots and various plants. For example, red dye was made from madder and waxwood, onion skins and horseradish leaves. Yellow dye came from goldenrod flowers, brown dye from walnut husks or butternut bark. Every home had its own recipes for making different colors and shades. The general store and the apothecary sold some dyes as well. Indigo, which came from the West Indies, was a popular blue dye.

Weaving and fulling

Once the wool was dyed it was woven into cloth on a loom. Hand looms were used for making scarves or ribbons. Large looms were used for making heavier cloth. When the cloth was made, it was *fulled*. The cloth was spread out on the table after it had been soaked in a soap solution. People sat around the table and pulled, pushed, and twisted the fabric. They kept the wool moving in a circle as they fulled it. In a couple of hours the material was shorter, thicker, and stronger. In some homes a frolic or bee was held for fulling. The wool was put into tubs of soapy water. Boys and girls danced up and down on the wool until it was soft and thick. After the fabric was fulled, it was sewn into dresses, pants, and coats.

Grandmother weaves wool into material on a loom.

This type of spinning wheel was called a monster wheel. It is easy to guess why it was given this name. But any woman who had to walk up to 30 km a day while working with the wheel would feel that she had put in a "monster" of a day.

Valerie finds that her apron comes in handy for many jobs. She is carrying lettuce in it to feed her rabbits. In the morning she collected eggs and carried them to the kitchen in her apron. Later she will use her apron to wave her father and uncles in from the fields for supper.

44

Linen from flax

Linen was made in much the same way as wool. It was spun, dyed, and woven. However, linen did not come from sheep. It came from a plant called *flax*. Settlers grew flax plants in the spring. The flax was ripe in July. It was then pulled out by the roots. The flax seeds were removed on a *ripple,* which is like a large comb. The flax was soaked in water and then allowed to dry. Bundles of stalks were then pounded with a paddle-like instrument called a *brake*. The brake caused the hard part of the flax to break off. The good silky thread was then separated from the rougher fibers on a *hackle,* which looks like a brush made out of nails. Hackling also straightened out the fibers. The fine fibers were spun into linen threads on a small wheel which was operated by a foot treadle. The thread was then dyed. It was later woven alone or with wool added to it. By itself it was linen. With wool, it became a fabric called *linsey-woolsey*.

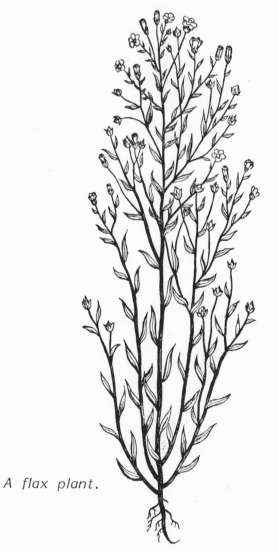

A flax plant.

Sunday best and daily dress

Cotton material could be bought at the general store or in a nearby town. Many people did not like cotton for everyday wear, because it caught fire easily if a spark from the fireplace went astray and happened to land on someone's shirt or dress. However, people did like colorful cottons for Sunday-best clothes.

Most people owned only two sets of clothes, one for everyday and one for Sundays. Women wore aprons over their clothes to protect their dresses from grease and dirt. Aprons were used to wave people in for dinner, to wipe one's brow and hands, and to dust furniture. Women also used aprons to carry wood, eggs, vegetables, and even baby chicks.

Patricia is on her way to church wearing her Sunday-best clothes. The people she passes admire the lovely cotton print from which her mother made her dress.

A quilting bee was a good way for women in a neighborhood to work and visit at the same time. Food was served during the day, but the women saved most of their appetites for the huge supper shared with their families.

The romance of quilting

Quilts were colorful bed covers made by women and girls. By the time a girl was old enough to marry, she would have made several quilts. The quilts were stored in a chest until she married.

The settlers did not buy special materials for their quilts. They kept every scrap of fabric that was left over from making dresses or shirts. When clothes had been worn beyond repair, they were cut into pieces to become parts of a quilt. The settlers threw away nothing.

Design was an important feature of the quilt. Designs were created by sewing together small scraps of colored material to form a larger patch. The design was repeated again and again until a woman had enough large patches to stitch together into one large sheet. This patchwork sheet was laid on top of layers of soft wool and cotton wadding and the bottom lining sheet. Women sat around sewing all the layers of the quilt together. Sometimes the children sat under the quilts and passed the needles back from the bottom to the top side of the quilt.

A big dance followed the busy day of quilting. The families of the women who were quilting were invited to round off the work with some lively music. Young men were asked to the dinner and dance so that they might get to know the eligible young ladies in the area.

The quilting bee

When neighbor girls and women gathered together to sew a quilt, the event was called a quilting bee. After the quilt was finished, the families of the women came for the supper, dancing, and games which followed. Quilting bees were one way for young people to meet each other. A young male settler had received an invitation for tea at a neighbor's house. He soon found out that every other young man he talked to had also received one. His father warned him about accepting the invitation!

"If several gentlemen receive an invitation to tea, they may be assured that their services are required at a quilting bee, *which often is followed by courtship and matrimony; indeed it is one of the methods taken by Cupid to trap hearts."*

Testing the quilts

After the quilt was finished, young people played kissing games as well as quilting games. Girls liked to throw the newly-made quilt over the head of one of the unsuspecting males and watch him try to wriggle out from under it. Sometimes they managed to wrap the quilt under the young man and with the help of many hands toss him high into the air. It certainly was one way to test the strength of the new quilt, as well as the character of the young man!

There was as much fun as there was work at a corn-husking bee. The man in the picture, above, discovers a colored ear of corn. This means he can kiss the girl on his right. At first she refuses shyly, but finally allows the eager young man to claim his reward.

Work parties

Neighbors were always ready to help each other complete difficult tasks. Together the settlers could do one job in an afternoon or a day. It might take a settler working alone up to two months to complete the same task. Working sessions were called *bees*. Bees could be organized to complete any task. All bees were carried out in a similar way. Neighbors were invited to come along and help. If a neighbor was not invited, it was considered rude of that person to attend. There were bees for every job that had to be done. There were barn-raising bees, logging bees, fencing bees, apple bees, threshing bees, spinning bees, stumping bees, and quilting bees. And these were just a few of them!

Lending supplies, tools, and hands

The people invited to the bee were expected to bring their families, their dishes, their animals (if animals were needed), and their tools. The hosts would organize the work to be done at the bee before the others arrived. The host family would also provide a feast for the workers and often music for the enjoyment of everyone after the work was done. One settler described the food served during the day of the bee.

The frame of the barn is up. The men take a break and admire their work. One of the workers places a branch on the top of the barn for good luck.

Good food for good work

"At eleven o'clock, cakes and pailfuls of tea were served round. At one, we were summoned by the sound of a tin bugle to dinner, which we found laid out in the barn. Some long pine boards resting on trestles served for a table, which almost groaned with the good things of this earth, in the shapes of roast lamb and green peas, roast suckling-pig, shoulder of mutton, applesauce, and pies, puddings, and preserves in abundance.

Supper was then served in the same great quantities with the addition of tea. After supper a variety of games and gymnastics were begun, various trials of strength, running, wrestling, jumping, putting the stone, throwing the hammer, etc. ...

About nine o'clock our party broke up and returned to their homes, well pleased with their day's entertainment, leaving their host perfectly satisfied with their voluntary labor."

A sewing bee.

Borrowing clothing was not usually considered proper, but there is an exception to every rule. Jennifer could not go to the school dance because she had no shoes. Linda came to the rescue by lending her extra pair to her friend. Both pairs of shoes received a good work-out from the dancing girls.

Borrowing

The settlers who lived in the backwoods far away from any town or village had to rely on the friendship of their neighbors. Sometimes they did not have the chance to go to the gristmill or the general store as often as their supplies ran out. It was common for neighbors to borrow from one another.

The most common items borrowed or lent were tea, sugar, flour, and medicine. All necessary things were happily lent to neighbors. When a neighbor had a *bee*, all the other people in the community expected to lend articles for carrying out the job at hand. Neighbors brought their pots and dishes as well as their oxen and tools. The hostess of the bee needed extra kitchen supplies in order to feed so many people.

It was a good idea to keep track of what and how much a person borrowed. That way there would be no hard feelings when the memory of the lender was better than the memory of the borrower.

The limits of lending

As a rule, to borrow clothing was not acceptable. One settler sent her daughter to a neighbor's house to borrow a night-cap, some lace collars, and a pair of boots. The neighbor refused to lend these things. She considered the items to be luxuries. Also, these things would not be returned in the same condition after being used. No one refused to lend something to a neighbor who was in need. However, when it came to luxuries, borrowing was no longer thought to be proper.

Although everyone expected to borrow and lend freely, settlers preferred not to stretch friendships to the limit. They did not want to lose any friends if they could avoid it. The old phrase "Those who go borrowing, go sorrowing" was useful to remind settlers of the limits of the custom.

The following story shows how some people borrowed much more than they were willing to return.

Naughty neighbors

"'My dear,' said Mrs. Stobbs to her husband one morning, 'the cornmeal we borrowed from Mr. Waite a few days ago is almost out, and we must bake tomorrow.'

'Well,' said her husband, 'borrow a bagful from Mr. Martin. He sent to the mill yesterday.'

'And when it comes, shall we return the cornmeal we borrowed more than a month ago from the widow Spence?'

'No,' said the husband gruffly, 'she can send for it when she wants it. John, do go down to Mr. Thompson's and ask him to lend me his ax to chop some wood this morning. Ours is quite dull, and I saw him grinding his last night. And James, go to Mr Watson's, and ask him to lend me a hammer – and you may as well borrow a few nails while you are about it.'

A little boy now enters and says, 'Father sent me to ask you if you had finished with his hoe, which you borrowed a week ago last Wednesday. He wants to use it.'

'Wants his hoe, child? What can he want with it? I have not finished with it. Tell him to send it back as soon as he can spare it again.'

They sit down to breakfast. 'Oh la!' exclaims Mrs. Stobbs, 'there is not a bit of butter in the house. James, run over to Mrs. Ritchie's. She always has excellent butter in her dairy, so ask her to lend me a plateful.'

After a few minutes James returns. 'Mrs. Ritchie says she sent you the butter, but begs you to remember that she has already lent you nineteen platefuls.'

'Nineteen platefuls,' exclaimed the astonished Mrs. Stobbs, holding up both her hands. 'That cannot be so. I never had half that quantity, and if I had, what is a little plateful of butter? I should never think of keeping an account of such a small thing. I have a great mind never to borrow anything from that mean creature again, as long as I live!'"

The general store was a great place for settlers to catch up on all the latest village news. While the men in the picture are enjoying a game of checkers, they also discuss community events. The small girl at the counter gets the latest report on the newest candies.

Keeping in touch

Day to day people kept in touch with each other by shouting to their neighbors to see if everything was in order. In many villages the church bells used to announce the death of someone in the community. The bells would ring out the age of the person who had died. Everyone would know of the death and pay his or her respects.

People would meet at the general store to hear the latest village news. The store-keeper knew everything that happened in the community. People dropped in at the store regularly and not only traded goods, but also traded news, political talk, and gossip.

Dropping in on neighbors was a part of everyday life in those days. There was always at least one person in the neighborhood who made it his or her business to mind everyone else's. People would visit the village gossip and be brought up to date on the latest happenings.

In later times newspapers provided people with community and world news.

The village gossip was always up-to-date on the latest developments. Above, she gives an eyewitness report on a broken arm. The victim stands beside her as she relates the blow-by-blow account of how the accident happened. The other children seem a little frightened by the vivid details of the mishap.

News from afar

The coming of the village newspaper kept the settlers informed about events that took place in other parts of the country and the world. Regular mail service helped the settlers to keep in touch with family and friends in other towns. Much later, the telephone made it possible to call on one's neighbors without traveling a long distance. The telephone party line would allow several families to speak and to listen to other conversations. "Mind your own business" had little meaning in the days of the settlers.

The telephone brought people together because this new invention made it possible for people to call each other from their homes. In another way, the telephone separated people, because it became easier to call on the phone than to call in person. ➤

When the Indian woman returned to the home where she had received shelter, she brought a gift with her. She thanked the little girl's mother with the gift of a beaded skirt.

Open doors, open hearts

Very few settlers ever locked the doors of their houses. People trusted their friends and neighbors. If strangers came to call, they were offered food and drink. They were asked to rest and even to stay the night. Sometimes travelers who came to a farmer's house late at night would curl up beside the fireplace and be gone again before the family woke up. The farmer might find a bag of flour or a piece of meat left as payment for a place to sleep.

In one case, four Indian women were traveling through the woods alone. It was growing dark. They knocked at the door of a settler's log cabin to ask if they could spend the night there. The settlers welcomed them and offered them a hearty dinner. After a good night's rest, the women continued on their way. A few weeks later one of the travelers returned to the log cabin. She was the youngest of the four Indians. She had made a beautiful beaded skirt for the woman of the house in return for her kind hospitality. The settler was amazed by the woman's generosity and thanked her for the wonderful gift. She did not expect to receive a gift. She welcomed all travelers in the same manner. She enjoyed the company of people who dropped into her otherwise lonely world. The two women quickly became close friends.

Ann wiped the forehead of the poor old man. He was so tired and weak that he could walk no farther. The settlers comforted and fed him.

Another settler told the story of an old man who came to her home. He was so tired and sad that she invited him in for supper and a hot cup of tea. The old man told of how he had fallen ill and lost his job in a nearby town. He was wandering the countryside looking for work. However, he was too old to learn a new trade and too weak to work on a farm. The settler offered the old man a bed for the night and sent him to her brother's farm the next morning. She thought there might be some work for him there. However, the old man never arrived. He died in the stagecoach halfway there.

The bad-mannered guest

Not all travelers and settlers were this friendly, however. (In every basket there is a bad apple.) One man came to a farmer's door and demanded a place to stay for the night. He threatened to burn the house down if he was not allowed to stay. The farmer showed him to a bed and then locked him in for the night. In the morning the farmer opened the door and asked him to leave. Instead of thanking the farmer for his hospitality, the ungrateful traveler left in a huff. He was angry about being treated as a prisoner rather than as a guest.

All the neighbors in the area met at the intersection. Their carriages form a long line up to the doorstep of their friends. The friends are surprised and happy about the party their neighbors brought with them.

The sociable settlers

Most of the settlers' social life took place in someone's home. People used every chance they could to have a party. Parties helped the settlers to forget the hardships in the new land and to remember the joys of friendship. Every job that required the help of others ended in fun and games. There were big parties around Thanksgiving and weeks of parties before and after Christmas.

Surprise!

People surprised their neighbors by bringing a party to their home. No one minded because the settlers would bring along musicians and plenty of food as well as guests. Surprise parties were very popular with the settlers. Several families would meet at an intersection and arrive together at one house. Everyone came and left in high spirits. Often the guests even tidied the house before leaving.

Wedding pranks

Weddings involved the whole community. Everyone in the area came to a wedding. There were several parties to celebrate the marriage of two people. Some were given by the parents of the bride and others by the parents of the groom. A favorite event that took place after the wedding was called *charivari*. The young men in the community would serenade the newlyweds with cowbells, tin drums, fiddles, and a great deal of howling. The boys expected to be invited inside for food and drinks. If the wedding couple did not invite them in, they came back each following night until they were received into the house for refreshments. If they were not successful in their plan, they played some rather nasty tricks on the bride and groom. In one case, a group of boys stuffed wet rags into the chimney in order to smoke the new couple out of the house. They nearly killed the newlyweds with their silly prank.

Everyone enjoyed a good party, and in the days of the settlers there were plenty of them. Almost any special occasion called for music and dancing. The people in the picture above are dancing off the huge meal they enjoyed after husking corn all day.

A wedding was celebrated with many parties. This party at the home of the groom was held a week after the wedding. The bride's parents had thrown many parties for the couple in the week before the wedding. Wedding celebrations took more than two weeks to complete.

Even the cold winter weather could not keep the settlers indoors. Families bundled up under the fur covers in their sleighs. Winter was the best time to visit friends because the sleighs and cutters could easily glide over the snow. These fashionable visitors will leave calling cards at every stop they make. If their friends are out, they will know that someone made a social call.

The calling card collection competition

As soon as there was a printing shop in the community, good use was made of the printer's services. In those days almost everyone had calling cards made. Calling cards were small cards with a person's name printed on each of them. Gentlemen usually carried small thin cards. A lady's card was larger. A young girl's card was smaller than that of her mother.

When gentlemen visited ladies at their homes, they left a card with one of the family members. On certain days ladies called on other ladies. Sometimes as many as twenty calls were made in a day. People kept track of everyone who called. If a lady was not at home, a card would be left to inform her that a friend had stopped by.

New Year's Day was a popular day for gentlemen to call on the ladies of a community. Cards were left on a table near the door. In the week that followed, ladies called on each other and compared the number of calls they had received by the number of calling cards that were left. It was a good chance for ladies to talk about all the men in the community. The men bragged about the number of calls they were able to make. Some men made a contest of how many calls they had made. Sometimes they even announced the number in the newspaper.

New Year's Day was a special day for the men in the community to call on the women. The entire Ames family is excited about the arrival of guests. Mrs. Ames receives the visitors as her unmarried sister, Ruth, hides shyly behind the door. Grandmother wonders if the refreshments she has prepared will be enough.

Happy New Year, Neighbor!

A glad good morrow! neighbor mine,
A good year to thee!
A year of life, and health and hope,
I pray that it may be.

Last year we held each other's hand
The self-same wish had we,
And has it not been well fulfilled?
Thank God! it has to me.

We did not wish that we might have
A summer all the year,
That winter's storms and autumn's blasts
Might never hover near.

And though they came – the rainy days,
Fierce storms, and bitter wind –
They passed, and left our sky perhaps,
More brightly blue behind.

So we will hope the opening year,
Whose morning is so bright,
May have a smiling dawn to give,
For every stormy night.

Willie is getting ready to make his New Year's calls. This is his first year for calling on young ladies. He will be going with his father and uncle. His mother is proud of the way he looks.

Each pew in a church belonged to a family and had the family's name written on it. Charle is pleased that his family's pew is next to Miriam Richard's, but in watching her, he forget to listen to the sermon! After the church services, the settlers will meet outside and chat with their friends. Perhaps Charles will ask Miriam to take a walk with him.

Jennie is learning to read from the Bible. As soon as children were able to read, they had to memorize the scriptures. The settlers faithfully read the Bible every day.

The church was one of the first buildings put up in a community. In towns such as the one above most people lived close enough to attend church at least once a week. The church was an important place for the settlers to meet and greet one another.

The Catholic settlers prayed together every day. In the picture, above, a family is saying the Rosary. The Rosary takes a long time to say because it is made up of 60 prayers. The beads are used for counting each prayer as it is said.

Children went to Sunday School every Sunday morning. In the afternoon after they went home they read the Bible. The girl in the picture, above, is bringing a new friend to her class.

Samantha plans her new home

Samantha Stell Adams was the young girl whose story you read on pages 6 - 11. She is all grown up now with children of her own. She married Joshua Adams, her neighbor. Joshua and Samantha have three children, Caroline, Phillip and Sidney.

A few years after their log cabin had been built, the Stells erected a large plank house near the lake. Their crops had brought in a good income and the family was soon able to afford a large, comfortable home. When Joshua and Samantha married, Joshua moved in with his wife's family.

Joshua did not want to be a farmer. He and Samantha had another dream. They built a gristmill nearby so that the farmers in the area no longer had to travel so far to grind their grain. Until then the nearest mill was day away. The new gristmill made the young couple wealthy in a short time. Samantha, Joshua, and their three children are now planning their new home. It will be Samantha's fourth home since arriving in the backwoods many years ago. Samantha's hard work has finally paid off!

Glossary

ammonia *a strong, colorless gas which is useful for cleaning*

backwoods *a thick forest where few people live*

barter system *trading one thing for another without using money*

borax *a white, grainy substance with bleaching power*

bran *the rough outer covering of grains such as wheat and oats*

breeches *short pants which end just below the knees*

buckskin *sheep or deer hide which has been tanned into a soft yellow leather*

cabinetmaker *a craftsperson who makes indoor furniture*

canopy bed *a bed with a tent-like piece of fabric draped high over it on a wooden frame*

chaperone *someone, usually an older person, who supervises the activities of young unmarried couples or groups of young people*

charivari *(pronounced shiv-a-ree) a prank played on newlyweds. The young men of a community loudly serenade the couple on their honeymoon night.*

communication *the exchange of ideas and information among people*

community *a group of people living in the same area, sharing resources, public buildings, roads, and interests*

divining rod *a forked wooden stick which turns towards the ground when it is held over a spot where water is likely to be found*

domestic *having to do with a home or household*

emigrate *to leave one country and settle in another*

fallow *an empty farmer's field*

finishing mill *a sawmill where rough-cut lumber was taken to be finely trimmed and sanded*

fireplace trammel *a metal device by which a kettle hanging by a hook can be raised above or lowered into a fire*

flax *a plant with thin stems and blue flowers used to make linen*

fleam *an instrument used to scratch the skin in order to allow a person to bleed*

foodstuffs *anything that can be eaten*

frame house *a wooden two-story house built of squared logs*

generation *a group of people with the same parents, eg. grandparents, parents, and children make three generations*

gossip *rumors and idle talk which people repeat to one another without proof that it is true; a person who regularly spreads such stories*

gristmill *a mill that grinds up the grain a settler has grown*

habitation *a place where people live*

hemlock *a type of evergreen tree*

hemp *a plant, the stems of which are used for making rope*

homestead *all the land and buildings that form a farmer's property*

hospitality *friendliness towards guests, visitors, and neighbors*

housewarming *a celebration held in the house that a family has recently moved into*

indigo *a plant used to make blue dye*

intersection *the point where two or more things, such as roads, meet*

lean-to *often the first shelter on a settler's land – made from logs strapped together in a flat surface against the wind, leaning on poles for support*

lye *a very strong liquid made from water and wood ashes and used to make soap*

madder *a plant with a root used in making red dye*

manufacturer *a maker of a product in large quantities, usually using machinery*

myrrh *a gum from trees used in perfume and incense*

needlework *work, such as sewing or embroidery, done with a needle*

orris root *a root from the iris plant used in perfumes, lotions, and powders*

pew *a church bench*

plank *a piece of wood sawed thicker than a board*

quinine *a bitter, colorless drug used to treat people who have malaria*

resin *a sticky substance from pine and other trees used in making varnishes and other products*

resources *things that are sources of help or wealth*

rheumatism *a disease that causes the muscles, joints, tendons, nerves, or bones to swell and hurt*

Rosary *a string of beads used to count the number of prayers said by Roman Catholics*

saltpeter *a white, clear chemical used to pickle meat*

sawmill *a factory where logs are cut by machines*

scriptures *religious writings in a holy book such as the Bible*

shanty *a roughly built cabin*

skein *a length of wool wound in a long, loose coil*

sod *the grass and soil forming the surface of the ground that can be lifted and planted elsewhere*

stile *a set of steps used for getting over a fence*

tallow *the melted fat of animals used to make soap and candles*

threshing *a process during which seeds are separated from a plant by beating it*

tonic *a medicine or liquid that refreshes or strengthens a person*

trundle bed *a low bed on wheels which can be rolled under another bed when it is not needed*

underbrush *small trees and plants growing under taller trees in forests*

valance *a short, decorative curtain hung around the frame made by tall posts of a bed*

Index

Acknowledgements

Library of Congress, Dover Archives, Colonial Williamsburg, Scugog Shores Museum, Port Perry, Century Village, Lang, Upper Canada Village, Black Creek Pioneer Village, Metropolitan Toronto Library, Colborne Lodge, Toronto Historical Board, Gibson House, City of North York, Harper's Weekly, Bibliotheque National du Quebec, Canadian Illustrated News, Public Archives of Canada, Ontario Archives, Frank Leslie's Illustrated Magazine, the Osborne Collection of Early Children's Books, Toronto Public Library, the Buffalo and Erie County Public Library Rare Book Department, Jamestown, Chatterbox, Little Wide Awake, Harper's Round Table Magazine, Book Society of Canada, William Blackwood and Sons.

12131415 LB Printed in the U.S.A. 987654